HARD KNOCKS

HARD KNOCKS

A REAL-WORLD EDUCATION IN BUSINESS AND PERSONAL GROWTH

R Mike Derryberry

Hard Knocks: A Real-World Education in Business and Personal Growth Copyright © 2019 by R Mike Derryberry.

All rights reserved. No part of this publication may be reproduced, distributed, or transmitted in any form or by any means, including photocopying, recording, or other electronic or mechanical methods, without the prior written permission of the author, except in the case of brief quotations embodied in critical reviews and certain other noncommercial uses permitted by copyright law.

Disclaimer:

The author strives to be as accurate and complete as possible in the creation of this book, notwithstanding the fact that the author does not warrant or represent at any time that the contents within are accurate due to the rapidly changing nature of the Internet.

While all attempts have been made to verify information provided in this publication, the Author and Publisher assume no responsibility and are not liable for errors, omissions, or contrary interpretation of the subject matter herein. The Author and Publisher hereby disclaim any liability, loss or damage incurred as a result of the application and utilization, whether directly or indirectly, of any information, suggestion, advice, or procedure in this book. Any perceived slights of specific persons, peoples, or organizations are unintentional.

In practical advice books, like anything else in life, there are no guarantees of income made. Readers are cautioned to rely on their own judgment about their individual circumstances to act accordingly. Readers are responsible for their own actions, choices, and results. This book is not intended for use as a source of legal, business, accounting or financial advice. All readers are advised to seek services of competent professionals in legal, business, accounting, and finance field.

Printed in the United States of America

ISBN-13: 978-1-945849-85-5 paperback
JMP2019.1

Dedication

To Cheri, my lifelong partner who has always been my greatest supporter.
To my father, Bill, who taught me to never quit, to always do it right the first time.

Contents

Dedication v

Acknowledgements 1

Introduction 3

Chapter 1: Know Yourself 7

Chapter 2: You are smarter than you think 19

Chapter 3: Play to Your Strengths 27

Chapter 4: Always Be Learning 35

Chapter 5: Systems and People. You Need Both. 45

Chapter 6: You Can't do this Alone 53

Chapter 7: People are Messy 61

Chapter 8: Entrepreneurship is Hard Work................ 73

Chapter 9: Change is a Signal, not a Problem 81

Chapter 10: Dream Long Term, Act in the
Short Term 89

Conclusion 97

About R Mike Derryberry 101

Acknowledgements

In life people enter and impact you in ways you don't really grasp in the moment. I have had several mentors over the years, and none of them are aware of it. I have read their books, watched their videos, and listened to their speeches, but never had the opportunity to say, "Thank you." I would like to acknowledge them now.

John Maxwell—from a speech at Promise Keepers and the many books that line my shelves, your wisdom has sustained and enlightened me in my most critical moments.

Patrick Lencioni and Jim Collins—from the teaching you have provided at the Global Leadership Summit to your writing and videos, I never go away with anything but a full quiver.

Simon Sinek—the power of purpose. I had no idea until you laid it out. Your research and empirical approach resonates deeply with me. Your insight has made me a better leader.

Jim Rohn—a man of compassion and common sense. I will listen to your teaching always.

Darren Hardy—You were the first one to help me see that a mentor can be anyone as long as you have the right perspective. Nuggets, nuggets, and more nuggets. Each truth has compounded over time and will continue to bear fruit.

Thank you.

Introduction

Initially I started writing down these ideas, or lessons learned, for myself. It was, and is, a way to process the ups and downs of the last 15 years in business, and to insure I don't forget those lessons going forward. Along the way I started sharing these lessons with other business owners and a consistent theme began to develop. Several struggles were common to each person I talked to, and in each case the lessons I had learned seemed to help them as well.

Recently people started commenting I should write a book. Normally when people say things like that I am inclined to be polite, but typically not follow through with that sentiment. However, one lesson I am learning is to not dismiss those comments and the opportunities that may arise out of them. Instead, pursue opportunities vigorously until it becomes clear this is not going to develop or, more importantly, it does turn into something I would never have thought about or considered previously.

In either case, I will have learned some new things in the process.

This book, then, is for those of us who are in the trenches grinding every day to fulfill an idea or a dream. We are not "Captains of Industry" or financial moguls, rather we are the 90% of all business in America, struggling to make payroll, agonizing over employee problems, inventory, customer service, and all the rest. We are the small business owner looking to make a dent in our universe. In short, I wrote this for people just like me.

At the outset I need to be very clear: these ideas, the concepts, and principles are not new. They are principles or concepts I learned from some very smart people. You could, as I did, read books, go to seminars, listen to podcasts, and then cull out what is relevant to your situation and apply these ideas, as I did.

So why should you read this book? Because, while you had the opportunities, just like I did, you are still looking for answers. The key is taking what you learn and applying it today. The question is, "Why didn't you apply those ideas?" Did it seem too much like theory and not enough practicality? Or maybe you seem so far away and detached from those people who offer such great information. I don't know, but I can tell you when I started listening and applying what they were teaching, I started to see progress.

Or, you dismissed the books and podcasts as interesting but not relevant, because in your subconscious you don't think that person speaking really understands your situation. I get it. But see, I'm just a small business owner grinding it out every day—just like you. So maybe you will listen to me and then act, because you can relate to me. Maybe you will relate to my experiences, or maybe you have heard this all before but this time it just clicks. Honestly, it doesn't matter. However you get the information and from whomever is not the important thing. Getting it, and applying it, is.

1

KNOW YOURSELF

> "One choice made or not, one small action taken or not, compounded over time will net huge success or colossal failure."

Why do you do the things you do? Is it for yourself? For other people? A cause you believe in? If you don't know the answer to that question you will face some very frustrating times ahead. I know, because it took me a number of years to finally understand the significance of knowing the answer. I had some pretty good business experiences throughout my life, but I also had a lot of frustration around those same experiences.

One of my biggest frustrations, from a business perspective, was employees just didn't seem to have the same level of "buy in" or commitment I did. What I came to understand, and this was a big "Aha" moment, was people couldn't read my mind or pick up on my thinking. I know, crazy, right?. It took someone asking me, point blank, "Why are you doing this?" and my realizing I had never clearly and concisely explained it or consciously formulated an answer in my own mind. Well, if I can't even explain why we do things, how can I expect others to understand and buy in?

My journey in this area was a bit backward. Please don't make the same mistake I did. My first introduction to this arena was a focus on my business and being clear about why the business needed to have a clear *purpose* (why) and clear *values* (how), not about me personally. One of my first big moments was at a large gathering of Infusionsoft users. Clate Mask and Scott Martineau, founders of the company, were giving the keynote speech. As I sat alone surrounded by 2500 other business owners in a large auditorium listening to them explain the philosophy they applied to their company, I suddenly became aware they were giving structure to some very disjointed ideas which had been running through my head. Finally! I remember telling a friend later it was like I had been doing my best to put a 1000-piece puzzle together without a picture of what it was supposed to look like. I had all the pieces, I just couldn't figure out how they fit together. In that moment I had the picture and all the edge pieces in place. I will never forget that moment.

People like Clate Mask, Jim Collins, and Simon Sinek helped me conceptualize not only the structure, but the very core philosophy behind this idea. If team members understand why the business exists and how we operate, they can decide whether they want to go all-in, or self-select themselves out. In either case, the organization is better off.

Even as we were structuring our *purpose* and *values*, it still seemed awkward and unsatisfying. The epiphany, for me, came as I was laying out an agenda for an annual strategy meeting. If it was so important for a company to do this, shouldn't I, a co-founder, know my own *purpose* and *values*? Amazingly enough, though my values were very ingrained in my subconscious brain and clearly determined how I behaved and dealt with issues and people, I had never written them out and coldly reviewed them or evaluated them the way I was evaluating my company. This was going to be more than a little uncomfortable. What if, once they were on paper, I didn't agree with them? Worse, what if they were shallow and not really worthy of being called *values* at all?

I spent several weeks writing down all the things I believed and held important. I wrote and edited dozens of times until I came up with the values, or what some might call axioms, that govern my decisions and choices. Many of them came from difficult setbacks and struggles. Some came out of deeply held convictions tested by time and circumstances. Over the years I have changed the wording or clarified the thought, but those values remain intact.

So, why do I believe it is so important to know your own values? Because your business, department, or organization will reflect you. My business has my values all over it. The business values, while slightly different in focus from my personal values, still have my values at their core. Yours will to. The big surprise for me was how our team reformed and reengaged. Because I was clear about my values, I was confident in and clear about the company's values, which allowed our people to invest—or leave—without judgment.

Knowing your *purpose* and *values* has one other benefit: it gives you fortitude and grit. When things get tough, and they will, you need to have a north star, a reason to continue, to stay the course. One of my *values* is this: *There will always be wind. Lean into it and keep moving.* If you don't, the wind will blow you away. We have faced our share of challenges, but we never quit. We keep moving until the storm breaks.

Having clear *values* is critical, but paying attention to the details is just as important. We have all heard the adage, *don't sweat the small stuff*. I have come to realize that is, or can be, absolutely wrong. It is the big stuff that usually gets all the attention. The big things are obvious, you can't ignore the big issues. However, it is the little, unattended or neglected details that will bring you down. One choice made or not, one small action taken or not, compounded over time will net huge success or colossal failure. At the time, standing alone in an isolated moment, it seems to be of little consequence. Except that one choice or action leads to another, and then another. The previous choice, thought, or action gives you permission to do it again, and again, and again. That is the danger of bad choices and careless actions.

It is also the secret to success. One action to improve your thinking, your relationships, your business plans—really any area of your life—gives you permission to do it again. Repeated, these small choices build new behaviors and then new habits.

One struggle we had from the very beginning was a sense of separation between the corporate office and our franchise owners. It was always a kind of *us vs. them* scenario. It seemed like no matter what we did, we couldn't break through to our franchise owners. A number of years into the business, I was reading a book that talked about the difference between leading and lagging indicators. The idea occurred to me that if we could identify one or two simple actions or behaviors, repeated over time (leading indicator), that would show we were one team with our franchise owners, maybe we could change the relationship. The one simple action we took was to have each member of our ops team simply call four franchise owners per week and talk to them about what was important to them. Not the business, not their accounts, and not any issues. It was to be about them and their families and their lives, not about us. Simple, right? We did not see any real change for months, but we kept doing this one little thing every week. About 18 months into the process I started hearing the franchise owners were starting to call us and tell us what was happening in their lives. The big complaint from our team was that the franchise owners wanted to talk for hours, which made getting work done a bit difficult. One little action, repeated over time, has made one of the biggest changes in our company. The little things matter.

The hard part of doing the right thing, making the right choice, is that you don't see any improvement in that one action, one thought, one choice. And boy do we need to see results. We need the reinforcement to feel good about doing it again. It's funny how doing the wrong thing doesn't have immediate consequences so we think it's okay to continue, but when we don't see immediate improvement from a good choice or action we immediately conclude we should stop doing it. That is just dumb, but we do it anyway.

I heard Brigadier General Becky Halsted say once, "Great leaders always choose the harder right over the easier wrong." The problem for most people is they make choices based on emotion and feelings rather than hard cold convictions. You didn't get a trophy or a pat on the back, so now you are going to quit doing the right thing. Really? When you know why you take actions and engage in behaviors, as Simon Sinek has so eloquently shown us, the conditions on the ground, right in front of you, become less stressful because you have made the choice without the emotion of the circumstances, well ahead of time, and the debate is over. It's time to act, to make the right choice.

I recently watched a video where a couple of farmers were going to take down a 50-foot-tall brick silo. It was hilarious, but also illustrated how little things can compound to create catastrophic results. These two geniuses thought this thing would come down with just a little "persuasion" in the form of sledge hammers pounding away on one side of the wall near the foundation of the tower. Time lapse made this much easier to watch. One hit after another over hours of hammering, chipping away at one brick after another. At one point they are exhausted and the base was over half gone, but, still no movement. They regain their energy and go after it again, eroding still more of the outer wall. Nothing. Finally, one guy in complete frustration, takes one huge swing and one brick falls out. Nothing. They start joking that this thing is sturdy. Suddenly without notice the tower wobbles and then crashes with a thunderous explosion, scaring these guys to death.

While this was funny to watch, the lesson seemed clear to me. Even the strongest structures can be brought down with small incremental blows to the foundation of a building, your business, your life, or a destructive habit. The small stuff matters. Sometimes we think we are invincible, that our businesses will not be like others before us, and meanwhile the base is being eroded by bad choices and outright neglect. The collapse is only a matter of time.

On the other side, incremental actions and choices can bring down negative attitudes and thinking, poor choices and behaviors, that are manifested in destructive habits. No matter how big the obstacle in front of you seems to be, steady, determined, consistent actions and choices can have monumental rewards.

If you would have known me in my younger days, you would have seen someone who was angry, critical, and not really the most optimistic person you knew. I had some family and friends who would comment on this, and mostly I would dismiss their comments, but partially listen. At one point an outside voice, of someone I respected, challenged me to make some incremental changes in my behavior. One of the most significant changes was to completely remove myself from listening to talk radio, news broadcasts, and reading daily print media. I determined to give this a test for thirty days to see what would happen. Those thirty days have now become six years and counting at this writing. What I discovered was that I was being influenced by the garbage I was allowing into my thinking. The time I had spent listening to news or talk radio was replaced with podcasts designed to improve my life. Without even noticing it, I started seeing possibilities I had not seen before. I actually started encouraging other people. My biggest discovery was that

I didn't need any of the information that I was now not listening to. One incremental idea, one behavior (among many), changed the trajectory of my life. I challenge you to test this idea for yourself. One day at a time and you can change your perspective on life. That is awesome.

As long as we are on a positive track and making changes, let me challenge you with one more. I warn you this one is not easy. I was listening to a podcast when I first heard this idea. My first response was, "Well that's pretty harsh." But upon reflection, I saw the wisdom in it. Have you ever thought about the people who influence you in the same way you think about the media that you absorb? People, especially those closest to us, have a proportionately greater influence on us than media, and yet my guess is you have never really considered a house cleaning in regard to your relationships. Jim Rohn used to say, "You are the sum total of the five people you spend the most time with." I would exclude (somewhat) your immediate family and then challenge you to do what I was challenged to do. Write a profile of the people closest or most important to you, by asking some questions. What do they spend their time and money on? What are their favorite activities? On a scale of 1-10, how would you rate their integrity, their faithfulness to friends, their trustworthiness? Can you trust their word as being solid? Do they have ambitious goals and dreams? I could go on, but you get the idea. Then ask yourself, *"Is that a description of a person I want to be? Am I comfortable with that description of me?* Your answer will give you a clear indication of what you need to do next.

In the podcast, the challenge was this: group all of your associations in three categories, those you will need to disassociate from, those you will need to limit your associations with, and those you should expand your associations with. Categorizing your associations is the easy part, beginning to disassociate or limit associations is the hard part. It took me months to migrate away from some people, others it was pretty quick, but it was never easy. The trick is to replace those people with those who will challenge you to be more and to achieve more. I purposely put myself around people who will hold me accountable and will not allow me to make excuses. It is uncomfortable, but it is so worthwhile. I am grateful beyond words to those people.

So, who are you? What are your values? What is your purpose? How would you describe yourself? Who is influencing your thinking, your attitudes, your behavior? Start making some incremental changes right now. You are smarter than you think. You can do this. It's never too late to start.

2

YOU ARE SMARTER THAN YOU THINK

> "Here is the reality: In most cases we have exaggerated the worst possibilities and totally ignored the best probability."

Stop second-guessing your decisions. Trust your gut. At one point or another we all have this moment where a voice inside of us says, *You need to do this*, and then we hesitate or make excuses. Hey, I've been there and done that. What I am learning is that while there are a ton of reasons (i.e. excuses) for not doing something or not acting, one of the biggest, at least for me, was self-doubt. You know how it goes, it starts with "I can't...," "I haven't...," "I didn't...," "They won't...", "I'm not..." Look, somewhere inside us there is a part of us that sees the potential in this idea, this action, but it is being overridden by all of our negative experiences and unknowns. These are all based in fear.

Fear will lead you to question your initial instincts. So, ask yourself, "What am I afraid of?" Most of the time it will be fear of embarrassment, the hit to your ego, or the potential of lost reputation. These are strong fears, but they are irrational. You will be embarrassed for a minute, your reputation will be in good company (see every great success story ever), and your ego will get over it.

A few years ago I had this crazy idea that our company could perform at a revenue level that only 1% of all businesses ever attain. I think it was partly my competitive nature and a need to prove to myself that I could do what others hadn't done. I started talking about our goals and posting them all over the building. Deep inside I was always a little fearful that things would blow up and I would have to explain all of my bravado. As it turns out, that is exactly what happened. We stalled and struggled to get back on track and I had to accept we had stumbled significantly under my leadership. But we also put it back together and started growing again. The amazing thing is no one cared. The fear had been all in my head. What is ironic is that out of that period grew a new goal, bigger than the first. My fears were unfounded. Here we go again.

To me, this is where courage is required. You may have heard the definition of courage as action taken in the presence of fear. Being in business requires courage nearly every day—at least it does for me. We get presented with opportunities every day, and most of them go unnoticed or ignored. We might look at something and think, *Wow that is a cool product/idea/concept/service. Maybe I should look into that.* But then we don't. It is that moment of inspiration where the doubt will come, and at that moment we need courage to act. Take a simple action to investigate it further, and then maybe a demo, whatever, but just start acting. It is the action that pushes down the fear.

Sometimes you need to remind yourself why you thought this business, this new job, this new challenge, whatever it is that has you so worked up, was so important in the first place? Write it down and review it regularly. You need this as your north star. Human beings have this great capacity to intuitively know when something is right for us, but we also tend to over analyze all the details, primarily all the things that can, and in our minds, will, go wrong. The reality is, however, in most cases we have exaggerated the worst possibilities and totally ignored the best probability.

Hard Knocks

When we first started in business I was afraid to take on big accounts because I was afraid of what we could lose. My gut told me that bigger accounts, customers who had an investment in their building and business, would appreciate what we were offering and how we were different. They would be partners and we could have a long-term relationship which would be beneficial to both of us. Sadly, I didn't listen to my gut and we avoided taking on bigger accounts for several years. Once we did take the plunge, what I thought would be the differentiator, in my gut, actually was correct. (Insert forehead slap.)

About a year into our business I noticed a technology that was being promoted in journals and industry marketing which I thought was going to be significant. But what I also noticed was very few people in our industry were adopting it. My gut told me this would be a significant trend in the future and would be a way to separate us from others in our industry. There was a risk we would make a mistake, that I really didn't know all that I needed to. I hate to lose, so this could be a big win or a big loss. In the end we chose to act in spite of the potential embarrassment, and we were right. Today that technology is being used almost exclusively across many industries. I used to say in defense of our decision, "Waves will come, you can either ride the crest or be crushed by it. I prefer to ride." This time we were right. Sometimes you are wrong. Regardless, give your intuition a little freedom. Allow yourself to be surprised.

One lesson I learned about acting on your intuition is summed up in a mantra I learned at a seminar put on by Infusionsoft's Elite Momentum. It goes like this: Dream Big, Test Small, Fail Fast, Learn Always. I have applied this process to almost every idea I have had since then. Here is the process as I use it. Take your dream or big idea and devise a small, controlled test. Identify a small group of potential users or customers and present the concept to them on a limited basis. Measure the results. If it was a good test, enlarge the test group and expand your offering. If it does not meet your expectations, this is also good news. Why? Because you did not waste considerable time and effort learning the truth. Instead, you paid for a lesson that will help you going forward, and you did so quickly. Maybe it is just a simple iteration that is needed. Test small again. Did it succeed or did it fall short? In either case, you learned something. The bottom line is you listened to your gut and you proved to your doubting mind that either you were right or you simply need to pivot. Either way, you win.

Have you ever been to a seminar or read a book, or even a blog, and a great idea came to mind? Did you act on it? Why not? I have been there. The part of our brain that is risk-adverse won the day. But I have learned you can change that scenario. Start by taking one small step. After all, you don't want to cause the part of your brain that is protecting you to freak out. Small incremental steps toward your idea will retrain your brain to move in that direction and take bigger steps.

I mentioned earlier I had some fear about taking on big accounts. I got over this by stepping out and taking on accounts that were 20-30% bigger and more complicated than before. We took on some larger chain restaurants and multi-location medical buildings. Without noticing it we were doing much larger buildings and taking on much more risk. So, what happened? Once we took on one account like this and didn't die, it gave my mind freedom to expand a little further. Success expands the border of what is possible. Small successes repeated over time become large successes.

Recently I was talking to someone about this change of mindset. When we first started the business, a $100 expenditure was a pretty big deal. We counted pennies, not dollars. Today that alarm doesn't go off until the expenditure is in the multiple thousands. We have—I have—created a new reality for my brain. Over time the part of my brain that protects me from harm has come to realize we can stretch and no one will die and everything will be okay. It didn't happen all at once, it happened one small move at a time.

You are smarter than you think. You have some great ideas. There are some new opportunities available to you. Don't let fear derail you. The point is, you have to do something. Emphasis on the *do* part. Start by playing to your strengths. Take action in the direction you want to go even if it is a really small step. Keep repeating the process, taking slightly bigger actions. Build some momentum and you will discover it isn't as hard to keep going as it was to start.

3

PLAY TO YOUR STRENGTHS

> "At some point you have to identify your strongest attributes and double down on those roles for the benefit of the company and for your own piece of mind."

Our business is a franchise business—that is, we sell and help people start their own business, within our system and with our help. In many cases those businesses are partnerships, either family members or friends. I have observed some interesting dynamics when two partners each try to be the main voice for the business. Most of the time it does not go so well.

Ironically my wife and I own our business together. In the early days of our business my wife worked a full-time job and actually traveled out of state during the week. This left me to run the business on my own. Nearly all the decisions went through me, so there was no real conflict. I was the accounting and payroll person, part time sales, operations, and cleaning technician at night. I did franchise sales, and when I had time, business owner. However, after two years my wife left that job to return to Phoenix and begin working full time in the business. The transition was emotional and frustrating for both of us. The transition took about two years for us to completely settle into our current roles (twelve years and going strong). We had to learn and unlearn some important truths about ourselves and each other. I have to say I had the hardest time with the changes. After all, I had made significant decisions and developed very strong relationships with vendors and our customers, and had been managing the business on my own. To have to give that up was like ripping out my heart. It was a shot to my ego and my identity.

So why am I sharing all this? Whether a partnership is a husband and wife, friends and family, or business acquaintances, the lessons we learned are the same. The lesson here is we all have strengths and weaknesses. Facing them head-on with some honesty is tough, especially if you were not struggling with those roles, and even enjoyed them to a degree. Why do we struggle with admitting we are not great at something? Why do we struggle with asking for help? I think it is because there is this myth that the founder of a company or organization is supposed to be this great super hero and is superior in all areas. We just "let" other people come along for the ride, but we really don't need them. I know for me it was more subtle, but just as damaging. I put the time and money into this. I did the research. I developed the plan. I took the risk. It was arrogance plain and simple. First of all, while I put the time in so did others. Yes, I did research, but I needed help understanding the information. Others took a risk by joining our young company. Every time we have struggled it is because on some level I have allowed myself to think much more highly of myself than evidence would support. We really are better when we can focus on what we do best and let others become their best.

My wife says repeatedly, "We have to play to our strengths." Here is the irony. While I was capable in some of those roles, I was not exceptional in them, and they weren't what I do best. They were however what my wife and others did best. At some point you have to identify your strongest attributes and double down on those roles for the benefit of the company and for your own piece of mind. When I finally came to grips with what I do best and embraced it 100%, I formed a new identity around those roles and discovered greater joy and success within the work I was doing. I was free to fully embrace my new roles without the encumbrance of all the other responsibilities. That was the moment we began to seriously grow.

So how does this apply to you? Of all the roles you play every day, which ones do you get excited about? Which ones would you do even if you didn't get paid? Where are you most creative? Okay, stop! You are putting too many things on the list. You can't do everything, and in fact, you shouldn't do everything. Seriously, stop and think about where you do your best work. Forget what needs to happen, just focus on the roles, the jobs you do, that you do better than anyone else and where you maximize your time and effort for the benefit of your company. If you are honest with yourself, like me, you will realize you are capable in many things, but exceptional in only a few. Find people, either within your organization or outside, who are exceptional at the things you are only capable or adequate in. Give them the freedom to be exceptional. Will they do it your way? Absolutely not, but that is the point. Your way is the best way you know how to get it done, and we have already established you aren't exceptional in this area. Get out of your own way. This is what I had to learn the hard way and what I hope you will embrace before it gets to that point.

Let me give you an example. I am more informed and have more knowledge in our operations area than anyone in the company, but I do not have the patience or the temperament to deal with the emotions that arise in customers and our franchise owners to allow me to be effective in that role. However, I have people in that department that are head and shoulders above me in this area. I am available to answer questions, but they are on the front line, not me. I am best suited to create systems and tools to allow them to do what they do best. When I spend my time doing those things they are more productive and the company is healthier. What is it for you? What do you need to step away from and what do you need to do more of?

There is a unique dynamic that happens when you bring in or raise up people and put them in roles that are best suited to them. When we first started adding new leadership I assumed if I was functioning as leader in five distinct areas, by adding leaders in those areas we would improve by five times. I was wrong. Really wrong. What actually happens is one person, focusing on one unique area, brings all of their energy to that one area and you end up with exponential growth in that area. It is not addition, it is multiplication. When I first observed this I remember saying, "Why didn't we do this sooner?" Why indeed.

So how do you determine which of those 93 things you are doing now are your exceptional strengths? There are assessments you can take, and coaches can sometimes give you direction, but honestly the people closest to you will be your best indicators. Just ask them. At first they will not tell you the truth. They don't want to hurt your feelings (believe me, the process is not painless). You have to keep asking specific questions, you have to keep on them and convince them you are serious. Ask them some questions like, "What am I doing when I am the most engaged?" "When do I become the most frustrated with you and others?" (suck it up buttercup, this ride is going to get bumpy). "When do I do my best work?" "What do I tend to finish and what do I tend to quit doing too soon?" When you ask these questions, don't take the first answer, drill down. "Tell me more about that. Can you give me an example?" The more questions you ask the more emboldened they will become, and this will be the good stuff.

You will want to defend yourself. Don't! As difficult as it will be, you need this information for your personal success and for the health of your company. Look, I told you this took me two years to resolve. Admittedly, I am stubborn and driven and sometimes overly confident, but it is a process. But what came out on the other side was absolute gold. Today I don't try to do what I am not exceptional at. I don't have to apologize for my less than exceptional abilities. I came to peace with my weaknesses and have embraced my strengths. That is freedom. It is life to our company, and it will be for yours as well. It is part of the process of always learning and growing.

4

ALWAYS BE LEARNING

"Your team is watching, and they are assessing your words and actions. This is why your personal growth and development are so critical."

You are your organization's most important asset. You set the standard for everyone else. Your team will look to you for all the cues of behavior and values. The level of your growth and development will be the cap on the organization. Lead by example.

Sounds trite, doesn't it? Here's the thing, trite or not, it is still true. There are lots of times I feel all my efforts are falling on deaf ears and our team isn't really getting it. And then they will say something or do something that is a perfect example of what I have been teaching. Your team is watching, and they are assessing your words and actions.

This is why your personal growth and development are so critical.

I remember when I first started teaching our team about our *purpose* and *values*. We would look at a core value or an aspect of our *purpose* each week, week after week. At one point I began to wonder if they actually understand how this influences every aspect of the business? A couple days later I overheard a conversation between two team members discussing an issue that had come up. I heard one say, "We need to take care of this today. We said we would do it, so we have to do it." Now, to you that might sound trivial, but you need to understand that one of our values is *we will do what we say we will do, when we say we will do it*. At other times I have watched team members jump in to help another team member complete a job even though they didn't have any direct involvement in the outcome. One of our other values is, *we work together as a single unit*.

I have to make a conscious effort to act and speak as I want my team to, because my default is to retreat to a quiet office and work on solving one problem or challenge or another. What I came to understand (over a long period of time after hearing multiple mentors convey this truth over and over) is that my most important job as a leader is to build my team, and I can't do that if I am running on empty. I have to keep learning. It was out of this lesson that ABL (Always be Learning) was born in my life.

A few years ago, I read a quote by Robin Sharma: "If you aren't leaving a trail of leaders behind you, you are not leading—your following." John Maxwell famously said, "If your leading and no one is following, you're just out for a stroll." My job, your job, as leaders in our organizations, is to learn and grow personally so we can raise our team's performance, both personally and professionally. When I finally got my head around this concept things really began to change, and not just for the company, but also for me personally.

So how do you keep learning? Read. Listen. Repeat. I read books, blogs, articles. I listen to speeches by the masters. I subscribe to podcasts. One thing I have come to realize is if I am looking for a nugget I can usually find it if I am open to it. What most people do is decide ahead of time whether the speaker or author is worth listening to. That is a shame. I have been surprised that at times even people who I do not fully respect will say or do something profound. I just need to be prepared to receive it. Even a broken clock is right twice a day. Tom Izzo, coach of Michigan State basketball, made a statement that pretty much sums this up. He said, "Learn to listen, listen to learn." This is essentially the definition of active listening. Everyone has something to teach us if we will just look for it.

There is one trick I learned several years ago that has helped me in this area. When engaged in a conversation most of us want to immediately jump in and offer our two cents when we hear someone else give an opinion. Instead, consider what the person just said and then respond by asking clarifying questions. That's the key, ask clarifying questions. Most people tend to ask questions to lead the conversation back to their opinion or point of view. If all you are doing is constantly returning to what you believe or know, you will never improve and never grow intellectually or emotionally.

Darren Hardy talks about asking questions as the process of mining for gold. This is a great analogy. Ask yourself, *Am I a successful miner?* Sadly, for most of my life I was not, but over the last decade I have made this a focus of my everyday life. I have discovered it takes at least two clarifying questions before I really get to the gold, and more importantly, they need to be open-ended questions, beginning with what or how. Who, when, and where questions are often necessary for basic data, but that is just fool's gold. It looks important, but it really isn't. Now, don't get the wrong idea, I am still growing in this area and I still revert to mining for fool's gold myself.

But when I stop and ask at least two clarifying questions, man, you can't put a price on that.

Here is a challenge for you. Over the next month make every conversation about the other person. Start by asking questions about what they are excited about and what plans they have. Make every effort to keep the conversation focused on the other person, not you. Ask questions about their answers. Turn this into a game. Do not volunteer information about yourself, but instead extract information from the other person. Why? This is a skill that will help you grow personally and allow you to potentially have positive influence on the other person. You will learn things that will be of personal value to you, knowledge you were unaware of, but also you will learn where the other person's strengths are, and if they are your employees you just might find a way to move them into a better position in the company where they can flourish and the company can reap the rewards of their improved performance. But you have to start by listening to learn.

They say knowledge is power, and if that is true, the more knowledge about another person I have, the greater opportunity I have to influence behavior and ideas. This is the essence of influence. Ironically, influence is what most people want, but they just go about it backward.

When I shift my focus from myself to other people and begin to ask questions about their ideas, they will become more open to mine. Ironically, pushing my ideas and opinions just alienates people and my influence is actually diminished.

One other side benefit of this habit is in the amazing relationships you will build. Why? Because when you are really listening and diving into what the other person has said, you are not focused on yourself, you are focused on the other person. And when you are that focused on someone else you will discover some very endearing things about the other person, including a greater appreciation for their point of view. Other people, those you are having conversations with, will be drawn to you, and that becomes the basis of a relationship.

Have you ever heard or read a great quote? A number of years ago I started collecting quotes. They were inspiring to me and I started saving them in a file to go back to at a later time. I know a lot of my mentors do the same thing. I've read their books and listen to them speak. What I didn't realize until later was how much those quotes would change my life. When I first started collecting and writing them down it just made me feel good to read them because I knew the meaning behind each one. I knew this because I would look into when the quote was made and the context in which it was made. The quotes were a simple reminder of a larger truth. Later I would recall these quotes in a conversation or when preparing a presentation. I even began devising axioms and quotes of my own to help remind me of a lesson learned or a circumstance I felt needed to be remembered.

What I didn't fully grasp was how much those little one-liners would ultimately impact my life. The more I used the quotes in everyday conversation or writing, the more those truths penetrated my thinking. The more my thinking changed, the more my choices changed, and the more my choices changed, the more my behaviors changed. And wouldn't you know it, my leadership improved, the results of my choices bringing major benefits to both my company and me personally.

So where do I get quotes? In short, everywhere. Let me give you an example. I was listening to an interview with Brig. Gen. Becky Halsted. She was talking about lessons she had learned about leadership from her leaders. At one point she sort of off offhandedly said, "Be your best, give your best, because those you lead deserve your best." As a student of leadership for years, that statement just hit me like a ton of bricks. I immediately wrote it down and memorized it. Today, if you take one of my business cards and flip to the back you will see that quote. At other times

I will be reading a book and a statement will just resonate with me. I won't just highlight it, I will write it down in a notebook. Sometimes I will be researching a particular topic and someone will have said something or written something I think is poignant or relevant, and I will again write it down.

Here is the key, though. Writing them down and putting them in a folder is only part of the process. You have to either memorize them or at least review them regularly. The learning process is subliminal and subconscious. You won't be aware of the impact until at some point in the future when you realize the truth of the statement has been integrated into your life. The change is subtle.

Here is an idea to try in your own office or building. I bought a 4-foot by 8-foot white board and mounted it in our office. I encourage people to write quotes on the board they have heard. Every so often we erase them and start over with new ones. Why? First, it gives me a subtle way of communicating an idea or concept to our team. Second, it gives our team an outlet to express their thoughts as well. Third, everybody wins, we all benefit from what one person adds to the board.

So, I have talked a lot about your personal and leadership development, but what about your industry?

Would you say you are an expert in your field? By expert I mean having an insatiable need to know everything you can about your craft and knowing it so well others come to you for the information they need. Are you still learning new things about your craft? Are you honing your skills to a master level?

I have been in my industry for fifteen years. I have learned a lot. In fact, I have had conversations with some vendors and quickly realized I knew more about their product than they did. Needless to say they aren't my current vendors. My point is not to be arrogant here. I spent a lot of time in classrooms, online, and reading to understand and become knowledgeable about my industry. I am still learning, still asking questions, and still gaining mastery of my industry. Why? That knowledge helps me more quickly and accurately make decisions about where we want to go next. It gives our team an advantage over the competition. When potential customers perceive you are more knowledgeable, their trust level goes up. When customers recognize you as the authority in your field they are more likely to follow your lead rather than someone else. Become a master of your craft, whatever that is. Be the go-to resource and you will always be in demand.

The big lesson here, *Always be Learning*. Become the expert in your field. Commit to improving as a leader daily. Now that you are the expert in your field, begin to build systems and develop people, because you are going to need both.

5

SYSTEMS AND PEOPLE. YOU NEED BOTH.

"No matter how good your systems are, you still need people to execute the system."

In 2006, a business acquaintance recommend I read Michael Gerber's book, *The E-Myth*. Since then I have recommended this book to anyone who will listen. I am inherently a systems guy. Process is equal to efficiency in my mind. What Gerber said resonated with me like very little before that.

When I was younger I worked as a plant manager, and one of the things I did on a fairly regular basis was break down tasks to analyze what was essential and what was not. I constantly wanted to find a flow from one task to another in a seamless fashion. My thinking was, the more we could gang steps together and simplify each step, the more time we could save and ultimately complete a project quicker. Fast forward two decades, and here was Gerber outlining the concept in a much more elegant and well thought-out fashion. I geeked out. Why hadn't I applied these principles to my current business like I had previously?

After reading *The E-Myth* we revamped our sales process, our follow-up process, and our customer nurture process and boiled them down to a very few simple and repeatable steps. I revamped our training program so every time someone new was trained it was exactly like the last one. We codified these steps and trained every new team member with the same process. What I noticed was virtually anything we did could have a repeatable system, and so we began the process of asking, "What else can we improve? Where are there inefficiencies that we have not yet addressed?" There is nothing more satisfying than when you create a simple and efficient system that actually produces results. I love systems, can you tell?

Our systems were, and are, a thing of beauty. No wasted effort, key communication is completed, results happen in a timely fashion, and repetitive activities are automated…most of the time. If I have learned anything it is that nothing, not even my beloved systems, are perfect. No matter how good your systems are, you still need people to execute the system. If people don't execute the system, well, let's just say things don't work so well.

But systems are also very freeing for people, because people are less worried about *what* to do and can give more attention to *how* to do it. When people are comfortable and confident that a process actually will work, they tend to relax and begin to express personal confidence and allow their personality to come out. In situations where customer interaction is involved, this is a huge differentiator. Your customers, my customers, want personal interaction, not a cold, efficient system. Your customers don't expect you to be perfect, but they do expect you to take responsibility and treat them with respect. Systems have no empathy, but people can have empathy and will show it if you create the right environment.

Having said that, you can't ignore the people side of business. In this age of social media, social and personal skills are suffering and, frankly, we need them now more than ever. When Gerber wrote his book, the business landscape was very different than it is now. The rise of social media, eCommerce, the internet advantage, and more, make doing business much more multi-faceted. Interestingly, it seems as though all of these new "advantages" have actually isolated businesses from the consumer. We discovered, and I am sure you have too, that the rise of social media and the social isolation that comes from it has created a decline in civility and social responsibility. Ironic, isn't it?

For us, this is an advantage. By emphasizing the person and restoring civility with our customers, we are becoming unique. Who would have ever thought treating people with respect and quickly addressing their concerns would be our unique selling proposition? Sad when you think about it.

Email campaigns, drip marketing, online advertising, online purchasing, while great systems, have almost eliminated personal interaction. As a company, if you can reintroduce the human factor, you can differentiate yourself from the competition. I can't tell you how many comments we get from customers when we actually respond in person to an email or phone call. They are surprised and stunned when they send an email, and within minutes someone is either calling them back or arranging an appointment to come and visit their business. Good people working a great system is the key.

Additionally, accountability and transparency are the glue that will ensure your people will execute the systems and plans you have developed. Just expecting people to know and remember what needs to be done consistently is not going to cut it. Years ago, I started repeating an axiom that has stayed with me and repeatedly proven to be true: You cannot expect what you do not inspect. People by nature tend to perform more consistently and with more dedication when they know they are being watched. Studies have proven this for decades. This isn't a mystery, so why, when it comes to your—or my—business, do we act like it doesn't matter?

I remember when I first became aware of this for myself. I was 19, working for a landscaping company, and had been given some responsibilities to build, install, and wire some electronic valves for a large job. This meant I worked by myself and apart from the rest of the crew for long periods of the day. On one particular day, a young family with a little boy, about six, were walking past the section of the job I was working on. They stopped to watch what I was doing. They were a little way off, but I could still hear them talking. The little boy was asking his dad what I was doing, and his dad was explaining it to him. As they stood there and watched I became aware of how focused I was on what I was doing and how important it was for me to do my job well. It wasn't that I was slacking off before they arrived, but my level of effort increased when they did. When people watch us, we tend to raise our performance. It is built into our brain.

Do you have a process that encourages your team, you, to focus on the important issues? Do you have a system for accountability? What you hold people accountable for is what they will focus on. This is not micromanaging, it is transparency. "What gets measured, is what gets done." Be careful what you measure, make sure it is important, of value, and make sure it contributes to your biggest and most important priorities. A few years ago I heard it put this way: "When performance is *measured*, performance improves. When performance is *reported*, performance improves dramatically. When performance is *reported publicly*, performance improves exponentially." I come back to this axiom a lot. In fact, it is plastered on our *Accountability Wall*, where our strategic plans and personal responsibilities are posted as well.

Every Tuesday morning our entire team meets to discuss two things: what we did last week to complete our major leading indicators, and what we are going to do this week to achieve our leading indicators. Our leading indicators are the activities we engage in to move the needle toward our three most important strategic initiatives. If you didn't complete your indicators you need to have a really good reason. But then we expect you to make up the difference this week. I say "we" because the whole team is involved and has a vested interest in achieving our strategic initiatives. If one person is not doing their part it impacts the whole team.

Accountability isn't just for our team, it is for the organization as well. One of the benefits of this weekly check-in time is to expose flaws in our systems which can then be corrected. Improvements in the system allow the team to actually perform better and achieve more. Transparency and accountability extend throughout the rest of the week and just become part of the culture. We aren't afraid of the accountability, it is what keeps us focused on the key initiatives.

So, do you have structure and systems that put your team in the best position to be successful? Are your systems designed to empower your team? Do they make life easier for your team? Are your systems netting real results, saving time, and improving productivity? Did your team have a hand in designing the systems? Is your team publicly accountable for their results? Have you identified key leading indicators, activities that have the greatest impact on your major priorities? Are you measuring and reporting publicly the results of your activities? Answering these questions is the first step toward building a balance

Hard Knocks

between systems and people. You need both. Just don't forget, you can't do this alone.

6

You Can't do this Alone

> *"The big lesson was that while we could lead and manage to a certain point, beyond that, we were the roadblock. We were restricting the growth. We were the problem."*

Okay, complete disclosure, I am a control freak. I like to be in control of everything in my life. In my mind I know what is best for me and what needs to be done in every situation. I am smarter than everyone else and can do it better than anyone on the team. Does that sound familiar? Hyperbole aside, if you are an entrepreneur or small business owner with drive and a dream, you are saying to yourself right now, "Yeah, what's your point?" Believe me, I get it. This is your idea, your concept, your invention, your baby, and you will protect it at all costs. But I am here to tell you that sentiment will kill your baby.

Hard Knocks

In the beginning, doing everything is pretty much required. You don't have staff and you don't have resources to hire them, so you default to doing it all yourself. But here is the problem, you are not only killing yourself, you are ensuring your baby will never develop properly. While it may be true this endeavor is your brainchild, if it stays yours alone or you try to run your employees this way, you are doomed to failure, or at the very least a minimal amount of success. You need other people to successfully reach the dream you set out to achieve.

My business is no different. After some initial bumps and bruises during our launch phase we managed to see the business grow year over year for several years, and then it plateaued. That first flat year I thought it was the economy, then I thought it was our competition. Needless to say, I was frustrated not knowing why we were stalled. Then one day it dawned on me, *we can't do this alone.* By "this" I meant leading effectively in multiple areas of the business, some of which were not my strong points. Now, I should have seen this earlier, the knowledge was there, I had been told this before, I just hadn't made the connection. We needed to add a level of leadership and give them authority to lead in their area of expertise. Easy, right? Not at all. I was going to have to trust other people to lead. I was going to have to trust other people to do things differently than I would. I was going to have to trust others to take our *purpose* and our *values* and convey that to the rest of the team on our behalf. My role was changing. My anxiety was going off the chart.

The transition was not all that smooth, and we had to deal with some bumps along the way. We attempted to promote people from inside first. We discovered pretty quickly they either were not interested in the role or were really not qualified to lead. We then decided to go outside to find those leaders. We made some mistakes there as well. In the midst of this drama I was forced to seriously reevaluate our hiring processes and reassess what we were actually looking for in leadership (more on this later). That was monumental. That was a huge lesson in leadership. Once we built the process and got clear on who we wanted in leadership, the process became much easier. We hired some great leaders and added some other support as well. It took us another year to build some momentum and turn things around. Was it worth it? Absolutely.

The big lesson was that while we could lead and manage to a certain point, beyond that we were the roadblock. We were restricting the growth. We were the problem. Once we got out of the way and brought in other leaders, everyone was freed up to become more productive and the company was able to start growing again. The illustration I used to use was two people holding hands around an ever-expanding tree. If the tree expands far enough the two people can no longer continue holding hands, and in order to allow the tree to continue growing more people need to be added to continue surrounding the tree. By not letting go and not adding more people we were constricting the growth. Lesson learned.

I mentioned this earlier, but it bears repeating. When you add leaders and give them the freedom to develop a given area, you are not just adding another team member, you are exponentially adding results. Why? Because they are not focused on a variety of areas like you have been, they are focused laser like on one area. That focus allows them to give 100% of their effort, time, and energy to that area. When they do, results tend to compound.

If you have read the book *Good to Great* by Jim Collins, you will recognize the illustration of a bus and passengers. Your bus is going toward a destination, and in order to get there you will need the right people on the bus, and more importantly, the right people in the right seats on the bus. However, I have discovered there are also "bus stops" along the way. These "bus stops" are key moments and stages of growth along the route to your destination. The challenge at each of these stops is that you are more than likely going to have to stop and ask certain people to get off the bus so that more qualified people needed for the next leg of the trip will be able to get on. This is not fun, nor is it comfortable. The people you ask to get off the bus are not bad people, they haven't done things wrong, but they are not able to navigate the next part of the trip effectively, and potentially could send your bus off course.

So where do you find the right people for the next leg of the trip? It begins with you, the leader. Knowing who you will need is critical. The tendency is to fill a gap left by the previous person. This is a mistake. You need people who can help you get from here to the next stop, which means they have either been there or have the advanced skill sets necessary. But before any of this happens you have to decide what the company and individual positions are going to look like. Those people will be completely different than your current team. Once you are clear about who, now you can begin to decide how to find those key players. We started with three key questions: How do you find the right people? Where do you find them? How will they be different from the current team?

The first thing I did was to educate myself about how to effectively evaluate candidates. I sat down with HR people from successful companies, companies that people *wanted* to work for. What questions did they ask? What was their process? What was their criteria? I also read books and talked to recruiters. I asked them how they filtered through all the candidates to find the ones best suited for a particular position or company. Ultimately, we created a basic plan we would use for all hires and then modify for each position. I stopped relying on my limited education and tapped into what others who are experts in their field were doing. Once again, I couldn't do it alone.

The answer to the second question, "Where did you find them?" is a bit more elusive. We used the online resources and we used recruiters, but the most effective source was networking—at least for us. I have discovered asking people you are connected to for their referrals of people in their network is the most effective source. We have less turnover and better success overall than other potential sources. I think this is because when someone is referring another person their reputation is on the line and it makes the referral very personal. Yep, you guessed it, you can't do it alone.

Finally, what is different about the current leaders compared to earlier leaders? I recently saw a sign that said, *Skilled labor isn't cheap, Cheap labor isn't skilled*. No truer words have been spoken. You are going to have to be willing to hire and pay for people that will take you to the next level. I would say, however, character trumps skill every time. I have hired skilled people but their character caused them and other team members a lot of problems. Skill without character and values that align with your organization is a disaster waiting to happen. Having people on your team that believe in your *purpose* and live out your *values* has to be your starting point. Skills can be taught, but attitude, mindset, initiative, a belief in the *purpose*, these things are internal to the individual. The possibility is that you can hire people with skills and then teach them the values. Anything is possible, but that is not likely. Start with the character of the person and then look for the skills.

During a seminar on hiring I learned a bad hire can cost you as much as three times their annual salary. I can testify to the truth of that statement. I have taken shortcuts out of desperation and come to regret it. I have been sucked in by a skill set or resume and ignored signals about character, and it has cost me the loss of business, the trust of vendors, and even other employees. I will never knowingly ignore the essential role of character ever again.

The obvious lesson here is, you need to be careful who you hire. While we need to include people, they can be messy. The most important thing I learned was that when you and your people do not have alignment of *purpose* and *values*, you will have problems. This may be the most important component of your hiring process. It was for us.

7

PEOPLE ARE MESSY

> "When you get clear about what you want and expect, and communicate that publicly throughout the organization, you give your team clear guidelines for behavior."

Have you ever heard the joke, "Business would be great if it weren't for people"? Anytime people, which includes you and I, are involved in any endeavor, things tend to go in ways we didn't expect and didn't prepare for. Every individual has an agenda, they may say they don't, but trust me, they do. And that isn't bad, you and I just need to be fully aware of that fact. Putting plans in place and assuming otherwise is plain foolish. People will not act the way you want them to 100% of the time. Get over it.

Hard Knocks

I have had more than one situation where I had mentored and worked with an employee and they were doing great, and then they did something completely stupid. You know, one of those things that your hand is forced and you have no choice but to let them go. Man, that is hard. I liked them a lot as a person, but their actions jeopardized our entire company. I hated it, I felt betrayed. It is especially hard for me because I have the belief that if someone comes to work for us they should leave better than when they came to us. I know people won't stay forever and I know that things happen, but still, I want them to be better when they do leave.

When people bail on us or do things we don't condone, we tend to blame them, but what I have come to realize is that often the problem was me. Many seminars and mentor admonitions went into this self-discovery. The problem would arise because in the beginning of our relationship I didn't clearly layout our values and associate behaviors that were consistent with those values. Or, I hadn't adequately modeled the behavior I wanted or the attitudes I expected.

Sometimes you don't have enough time to model the attitudes and behaviors—no, wait, you do have the time, you just haven't seen the value or benefit in spending it this way. Seriously, if you aren't spending a significant portion of your time pouring into your team, you are quickly setting yourself up for some major headaches. If you want more consistency throughout your organization you have to be clear about the organization's *purpose* and *values* and their coinciding behaviors. Do you have a process or structure for communicating these to your team? Do you have a systematic way of teaching and reinforcing your *purpose* and *values* throughout the organization? Take some responsibility for not communicating clearly to your team—after all, if you aren't teaching them these values and behaviors, who will? Yes, you do have time. Jim Rohn once said, *"Learn to help people with more than just their job, learn to help people with their lives."*

When I first started this process with our team I have to admit it was clunky and pretty rough, but we started anyway. My first step was to make sure I understood not only our corporate values, but the reasons why the process of developing them was important. We then engaged the whole team. We only had eleven employees, so it was a bit easier to include everyone at once. If your team is larger it might be easier to do this one department at a time. We got their input in a sort of free-form discussion, and then did some wordsmithing to include as much of their feedback as we could. When you include your team in the process they will take ownership of the results and you will solidify buy-in from them. You cannot replicate this in any other way.

What came out of the process were eight behavioral statements we believed described how we conducted our business and what we expected, when we were at our best, of our team members, customers, and vendors. So why was this important from a people perspective? For the first time we publicly were committing ourselves to a set of beliefs and behaviors that would identify us and those we would do our best work with. While some of the original team have moved on, the current team members are clear about how we conduct ourselves and who we want to do business with.

When you get clear about what you want and expect and communicate that publicly throughout the organization, you give your team clear guidelines for behavior. It will allow you to filter out those employees whose values are not in alignment with the organization. Does this sound harsh or cold? Believe me, it is not. You are doing people a favor. Misaligned people are typically not happy, satisfied, or fulfilled, because everything around them is contrary to their values. They aren't necessarily bad people, they are just operating with a different plan. Release those people—for their sake and yours.

The other side of this coin is how this impacts the new team members that will come onboard. When you are clear up front and evaluate people based on the *purpose* and *values* of your organization, you are less likely to add people who are misaligned. As I mentioned earlier, making a bad hire can cost your company dearly, not just financially but in lost time and opportunities. Before we got clear on the character issue we basically hired people based solely on our first impression and their work history and supposed skill sets. Well, you can't verify skills without some tests, and first impressions are not an indicator of future compatibility or performance. You have to be fanatically intentional about vetting people. Our biggest mistakes have come when we were not intentional, and frankly, lazy about our assessment of a candidate.

I don't know who said this first or where it originated, but the first time I heard it was from Darren Hardy. In talking about his team values, he made the statement, "Hire patriots, not mercenaries." Patriots believe in the cause, your corporate purpose, mercenaries believe only in self-interest. When I heard this I immediately resonated with it. I think you will to, especially if you are serious about your organization's *purpose* and *values*. The challenge, of course, is how do you screen for patriots and pass on the mercenaries?

I think part of the answer is what I eluded to earlier. For us it is about the behaviors that naturally flow from the values we view as critically important. Start by writing your values out in terms of the behaviors that best exemplify that value. Let me give you an example. We believe in personal responsibility, so our value is stated as, "We are accountable for our actions at the moment we act." It is important to associate behaviors with our values because people are not left to interpret a value, it's clear. This is very useful when you have to coach an employee. The value-behavior is clear, and when their behavior contradicts the value-behavior your conversation is around changing attitudes or conduct not about their value as a team member or their worth as a person.

Once you are clear about the behaviors you expect, you can craft questions that will help you identify similar behaviors in their past experiences. How did they act in a given situation? Who did they get involved in that situation? How did they handle the outcome? Your values will determine the best questions for your organization.

One of the greatest advantages of testing everything through the filter of your values, to your organization, comes in those difficult times when you have to let someone go. This is the hardest part of being a leader, owner, or manager. How do you separate the person from the performance or the behavioral issues? When you set clear expectations up front, both in terms of performance and behavior/attitudes, you can address those issues from a non-personal perspective.

> *"John, our values state we are all going to strive to achieve the best result in every situation. What we have seen is that you cut corners and show a disregard for team members and customers. We are consistently left to deal with issues that are not ideal."*

You will notice we are not attacking John's character, we are addressing clear behavioral issues that clearly violate our *values*. Obviously this is a bit contrived and we would do a lot of coaching early on to prevent a dismissal, but the key point here is our focus is on the behavior not the person. Believe me, when I started using this model for coaching and discipline the tone of my conversations changed dramatically. It was no longer personal. The other person can detach their emotions and focus on the behavior, which they have absolute control over. Ambiguity is what causes emotions to get out of control, clarity about behavior diffuses all of that.

The big lesson in all of this is that whether you are hiring, coaching, or firing, it needs to be done around behaviors that contradict, or align, with your stated values. People understand clear behaviors, these are visuals they can get their mind around, something they can see modeled by others, or something they can emulate.

So let me guess, you like being the boss because you like telling people what to do, and you could care less if they like you. Uh, no. If you are that kind of "leader" we need to have another kind of conversation. In most cases, my guess is that you are just the opposite. Your problem is not that you are being too hard and uncaring, it is that you don't like conflict, you want to be liked by everyone, and you secretly hope they will somehow see the error of their ways and change their behavior.

I have some bad news: it won't happen. As a caring leader you have to sometimes step into what I call "Difficult Conversations." You will have to face conflict, you won't be universally loved, and your employees will not change behaviors without your (or your leadership team's) intervention. But here is the good news. When you have been clear up front about behaviors that are aligned and those that are not, the interactions you have with your team will be much more effective. Keep in mind you are the guardian of your company, you have a fiduciary responsibility to protect the organization, and one person's behavior cannot derail that.

A process I learned several years ago has helped me stay on track and focused even when situations get a bit tense. Here is what I do, maybe it will help you. First, I never go into a conversation like this before I have thought it through. Second, identify what is the exact behavior that is inconsistent with your core behavior-values. Often times I have discovered that in doing this I discover it really wasn't a behavior or attitude that was the problem, it was my unwillingness to accept this team member was performing his or her duties in a way I would not. It was about me, not them. At this point, case closed. In other circumstances it is about a misalignment. But now I am focused on the behavior not the personality. Your focus has to be on the issue, the value-behavior, or performance, never about them as a person. A side note here, make your aim to restore the team member and to help them improve. A friend of mine once said this in relating a situation in her business: "Firing you would be easy, instead you and I are going to work to correct this." I love that because it says to the team member, "You are valuable and this is a team effort." It puts the emphasis on improvement and the work that needs to be done.

This brings me to the third step. Determine ahead of time what the best result would be, and then when you have the conversation with your team member allow them to tell you what steps they are going to take to achieve that result, with your guidance of course. As long as the outcome is values-based and not your bias, the result will be positive. When you make the team member define the steps, you have made them the owner of the outcome, for good or bad. Giving your team ownership of the outcome empowers and motivates them in a way you will never be able to. At the end of the day, they either own their success or failure. This never becomes a personal conflict between you and the team member.

I am ashamed to admit this concept is a relatively recent discovery for me. In the early days I was not clear with the team about my values or my expectations. They were all in my head, and often times people would act in ways that violated those internal value-behaviors, primarily because they didn't know what I expected. I coached poorly, if at all, and so, often times conflicts arose and neither of us was a winner. As a leader, I was immature and felt like this was my company and my way. It was very humbling, and a revelation, when I came face to face with my lack of intentional leadership.

Once I fully embraced this concept and applied it tirelessly, things turned around. We still have people leave, but not before we have done everything possible to salvage the situation. No system or process is flawless, but I have found this three-step process helps bring focus and clarity to a situation and removes personal feelings and emotions, which allows for a positive resolution.

I wish I could tell you this is easy or you can learn this quickly, but the reality is being an entrepreneur is hard work. But, hey, if it was simple or easy you wouldn't be unique.

8

ENTREPRENEURSHIP IS HARD WORK

"Don't confuse hard for wrong. If your business is hard work, don't assume it is the wrong business."

Anything worthwhile is worth working for. When I was growing up I seem to recall hearing that adage all the time. I have to admit I hated that. Why can't something be easy? As I grew up I realized that adage was more true than I wanted to accept. What I discovered was if you didn't earn it you didn't care about it and didn't value it. Fast forward fifty years, and it is more relevant today than ever before. Most people don't really want to put the effort in to achieving success. When I was growing up I never got the option to quit, and it became part of my personality. When I was in college I had a mentor tell me he had rarely met anyone with my level of tenacity. I wasn't sure if that was a good thing or not. Honestly, I didn't know how to quit, you always finished whatever you started. For me quitting is not an option. Maybe it's my upbringing, or my ego, or my aversion to losing, but you just keep at it. Success won't be given to you, and it won't come easy, it will only come from hours and hours of hard work. But it will be worth it.

So much of what we do in business is not like the fairy tales of Silicone Valley. Here is the reality folks, most of the time business is a grind, it is hard, and at times just plain boring. It is in a word, mundane. Unfortunately, too many people don't grasp that. Frankly, I think it is a test to see who is worthy to be in business and to make a go of it. Okay, maybe not, but if you cannot get your head around the effort that is required to make your business a success, get out now. Too many young idealistic entrepreneurs don't want to hear this. Welcome to the real world kids, it's called work for a reason.

You may have heard the quote, "Do what others won't, so that you can have what others don't." If the shoe fits, start wearing it. Look, being a business owner is not for the faint of heart. The vast majority of people want to have their own business, but having to do the hard work turns them away. I hate to break it to you, but there are no quick fixes, no shortcuts, and no one is going to do the work for you.

If you are reading this then you already know all this. My point to you is you aren't alone. All of us in this crazy entrepreneur world face the same grind. It is the price of admission. I would challenge you to find some other business owners you can talk to about any of the stuff you are going through. What you will find is a common understanding and support. Recently, I was talking with another small business owner and he confided in me he was so frustrated he just wanted to quit. That just kills me. We need more business owners like him, not less. I did what I could to give him some new ideas and encourage him to keep going, but ultimately the choice will be his.

The rewards come after the long hours and the sacrifices. It is unfortunate the media promote these superstar entrepreneurs and hold them up as what can happen if you launch out on your own. Yes, there are some that have a great product, software, or service at just the right time for the marketplace and it seems like they didn't do anything that required a lot of effort. What they don't really emphasize is all of the hard work that went into getting to that point. The success and the notoriety are the reward for all the hard work, the same work you and I are putting in right now. If you are at a place where you are just ready to throw in the towel and be done, please don't. We need you to stay in the game, it's not over yet.

Too many people quit before the good stuff. Not you, not today. Over the years I have heard this illustration, and maybe you have to. Have you ever used a hand water pump, the kind you might see on old Western movies? If you have, you know getting the water out of the well, up the pipe, and out of the spout is tough work. In business we do the hard work, but sometimes we pump and pump and we think since no water is coming out something is wrong. Maybe this is the wrong pump or the wrong location, when in reality it's just going to take more pumping. In some cases we pump long enough to start seeing some water come out. Not a lot, but enough to give us hope. We then determine the amount of water coming out is not worth the effort, and we quit. Some continue to pump and discover the water flow eventually turns into a nice steady flow that takes very little effort to maintain. In this illustration we can see the stages in our businesses. It's hard at first and seems to take forever, then a little success which seems like too little reward for too much work. But when we push forward we become the "Ten-year overnight success story."

Don't confuse hard for wrong. If your business is hard work, don't assume it is the wrong business. Why did you start it in the first place? What made you want to do this? Write it down and tape it your wall or mirror and read it often. Make a commitment right now to not quit, not give up. Keep pushing for success. The other side of that coin is this: if you can't remember why you started this and you have no idea why you wanted to do it, then maybe you do need to look for an exit plan. But don't be too quick to bail, you just might be tired and fatigued. I will tell you what has worked for me, other than a vacation, is to start talking to other business owners about their business and why they do what they do. They will remind you of your original purpose as you hear their passion for their business. I do this regularly to keep that fire burning and my vision focused.

How many times have you heard something like, "Find your passion and go for it," or, "You have to love what you do or find something else."? There are a hundred variations of the same idea. If you take this idea to its ultimate conclusion you will bail out on literally everything you do at some point. I don't love my business every day. I don't. But, I am fully committed to my purpose for doing it, and that is what drives me. This notion that you somehow have to be on this emotional high every moment of every day is not realistic and not sustainable. There are dozens of aspects to my business and yours that are just not fun, but they are necessary and essential for success. Make sure you are clear about the distinction I am making. I absolutely believe you must have a passion for what you bring to the marketplace or the world at large. You must be 100% committed to why you do your business, but don't confuse that with being passionate about the actual day to day work.

The day to day work can be a real blast...some days. When things are clicking and all systems are working together and you are producing, man that is an adrenaline rush. But sometimes outside factors influence our ability to produce, and things just don't go smoothly. So now you are going to quit? Please, it's part of the ebb and flow of business, not an indicator that you are in the wrong business. Our business has faced bad reviews on social media, financial struggles, and employee misbehavior. Each member of the team has been pushed to their limits and we have faced frustrations with each other and customers and vendors. But we are still moving forward one step at a time. It's what you do to achieve your desired level of success.

Some of the biggest and most difficult work you face will center around changes, but change can be a signal for an opportunity, not necessarily a problem.

9

CHANGE IS A SIGNAL, NOT A PROBLEM

> "Change can be, and usually is, a signal that we need to iterate and adapt. Those who do so first are the leaders, the rest will follow."

Are you comfortable with change? Most people say they are, but what they say and how they actually respond when change happens are two different things. The kind of change that can really slam a business is the change that happens outside of your control. I don't know about you, but I love change as long as I create it and I control it. When change disrupts my plans or sends me in a direction I am not comfortable with, well, now we have a problem. I used to get frustrated because I put all of this work into my plans and somebody came along and disrupted them. What I have learned since then is you can take control of the change and use it to your advantage.

It has been said you can't always control what happens to you, but you can control how you react to it. If you intentionally take time to evaluate your landscape and honestly observe what is trending in your market, you can anticipate what is coming. In this case, you get to be the change agent. You get to control the change. You get to initiate how you will adjust to it. This anticipation will allow you to iterate your business or do a complete pivot.

Change can be, and usually is, a signal that we need to iterate and adapt. Those who do so first are the leaders, the rest will follow. When we started our business, the majority of our competition were operating like they had for decades, and not really knowing better, we were following suit, doing what the majority were doing. I didn't recognize it at the time, but we were about to learn what is meant by the "herd mentality," where everyone follows the same direction so they can fit in. Either dumb luck or inexperience led us to make different choices than most of our peers. We did some things differently, we looked for other ways to accomplish the same results, but with better efficiency. Technology was our comfort zone, so we gravitated in that direction and adopted technology that was not widely used in the industry and adapted it to our needs.

It appeared to us that technology, at least current technology at the time, was something that many of our peers were either unable or unwilling to embrace. We had established the business using the same methods and processes our competitors were using, so we were technically in the same situation they were. In all fairness, because we had come from technology backgrounds, embracing technology of all kinds was an easy choice for us. Technological changes were coming, and either you were going to integrate the changes or get consumed by them. We were new to this industry and I had a fear that if we don't change and iterate, we are going to lose this whole thing. Maybe our inexperience was our advantage. After all, we didn't have years of history doing things one way, and clearly we weren't married to the existing norms. We just wanted to be distinct and keep up. What I learned was change can be a signal that there is an opportunity right in front of you. Unfortunately, most people view change as a threat or a problem to be avoided or defeated. We saw it as a way to be different.

It is hard for us looking back now, but things like online customer portals and online forms are really not that old. Back then there were a few CRM programs, but very few and not very affordable by today's standards. Some were using DOS programs, and online meetings were just starting to become a real option. We decided online programs and equipment technology were going to be our edge. I went to every educational seminar offered. I wanted to know what technology was coming out, what would help us be more efficient. It seemed like as soon as we adopted one new technology something else would come out, or something in another field looked like a possibility for our field. Throughout this whole time one truth was clear: change is constant and it is happening faster all the time. You need to get comfortable with change.

Adopting new technology or ideas or methodology is stressful, no doubt, but not adopting them can be lethal to your business. There are a couple of ways to look at change. You can say, "Change is unproven, so I am going to wait," or "Change is happening, how can I use this to my advantage?" A quote I have come to really love is one I heard from Alan Molaly, former CEO of Ford Motor Company. He said, "Instead of asking what is the right choice, ask how can I make my choices right." Embrace the change and make it right as you go. Waiting never served anyone looking to make a difference.

Netflix is one of my favorite examples of adaptation and pivot. They began by looking at a change in the market and building a system and business to address what they perceived to be a void in the market. They were right. Over the years they have iterated constantly. They initially saw there was an opportunity to develop subscription-based video rental. When it became clear streaming was going to be the new delivery vehicle, they systematically phased out the mail order portion of their original business and went to streaming. Then the next pivot came when they saw that original programming was a big draw. Do you know how many companies are today copying their model and doing the same thing because of Netflix's success?

There is another side to change that is disconcerting and amusing at the same time. Several years into our business I began to notice the majority in our industry, and probably yours, known as conventional wisdom, are usually slow to adapt to change, and in some cases downright resistant. I heard someone make this observation about conventional wisdom once: "If the majority of people make up conventional wisdom, and the majority of people are average, doesn't it make sense to do the opposite if you want to be more than average?" I am amused by this because I have observed it for myself dozens of times.

I guess on one level it makes sense, there is a perceived safety in the herd. You know, safety in numbers. I guess in the animal kingdom the herd provides protection from the stronger predators, but that begs the question, do you want to be a part of the herd or the big cat roaming the Savannah doing his or her thing? By its very nature the idea of the herd is that you aren't strong enough to go it alone. This isn't the animal kingdom, and eventually someone in the herd will get picked off. Nothing new ever happens in the herd. There is no independent thinking. There is no new thinking. You aren't an animal without cognitive abilities. You are not powerless and weak. You do have a brain and you can be unique. Don't be average.

Fortunately, there are many people who are not interested in the herd and would rather explore other options. These are the innovators, the people who aren't satisfied with the status quo. I wouldn't say our company are innovators in the truest sense, but I really like the idea of finding a better solution to an existing problem. I like the curiosity factor, the experimental element. I like the problem-solving aspect. I'm always thinking, *What if this works?*

It has been said the seven deadliest words of a dying organization are, "We never did it that way before." That is the herd mentality to a tee. The disconcerting part of this is that if the herd rules, progress is at the least slowed, and possibly shut down all together. What I have learned is if you educate yourself about the changes you are facing, and you know your business well, you can iterate intelligently and have success. Honestly, if you don't iterate regularly you are in danger of becoming irrelevant. I don't want to be irrelevant, do you?

The challenge for us is to observe the change, ask enough questions to clearly understand the changes and how they will impact us, and then, with that information in hand, plan and leverage the change to our advantage. It is business judo. And yes, this is work, essential work, for the health and future of your business. It can't be done once, it has to be ongoing. To think you have it all figured out and you will never have to worry about that again is delusional. It is your job, my job, as leaders of our companies, to stand on the wall and see what is coming, and then pivot. Use the change to your advantage.

I'm not saying change or adopt something new every ten minutes. You need to be smart, informed, but not frightened about change. Investigate, ask questions, test small, keep learning. Ask questions like, "Does this separate us from our competitors?" "Will this help us serve our customers better?" "Does this add value to our current service/product?" If you answer yes, it is worth

Hard Knocks

the risk to jump in. I challenge you to be the next change agent, especially for your company. Dare to dream in the long term, but act in the short term.

10

Dream Long Term, Act in the Short Term

> "Goals are the markers that tell us whether we are on course or not. Goals give us a benchmark to know if our activities are helping us or hurting us, but by themselves they are pretty much useless."

Are you a goal setter? Do you have dreams about what could be? I really hope so. Having a vision of what can be is what gets us up and out the door every day. How far away is that dream? How detailed is it? If you were to describe it to me, would I have a clear picture of what your business would look like when you get there? Who would you be serving, who would be on your team, what would they be doing, how would your company be perceived in the marketplace, what would be your reputation? The point here is, do you have a clear vision of what your end result is going to look like, and is it so real to you that when describing it to me, I could actually see it, smell it, and taste it? Yes? Very cool. How are you going to make that happen?

A dream or a vision is motivational and even inspirational, but it isn't enough. Goals and dreams, in my mind, are very different. Dreams are feel-good pictures or perceptions of what could be, even will be, but they really don't have a concrete nature to them. No deadlines, no specifics, no plan. Goals are all of that, they are the other side of the coin. If dreams represent the final destination, goals are the maps and reference points along the way. Goals are the tools to get us to our dream.

I like big goals. Smaller goals seem like a waste of time. If you just have to put a little more effort into your project or business, or work a little harder to achieve the goal, then I have a question for you: Why aren't you doing that now? No, really, why aren't you putting in the extra time, making the additional calls, taking the extra classes?

The dangerous part about goals is we set them just a little farther down the road so we can actually achieve them and feel good about our success. But what if your goals were so big it was impossible to achieve them without fundamentally changing every aspect of your business? What if my goals were so massive I would be embarrassed to tell people publicly? It takes as much work to have big goals as small ones, so why not go for big? When we set goals our brain (reticular activators) starts looking for opportunities to achieve that goal, so it makes sense to have bigger goals, which would lead to bigger opportunities.

So let me ask you, what do your goals look like? Are they specific, are they measurable, are they attainable, relevant and time-bound? No? Well then we have some work to do. What I have just described is what is known as a SMART Goal. Let me break down how I understand and apply this common acronym.

Simple. We have all heard the acronym KISS, Keep It Simple Stupid. I am not calling anyone stupid here, the point is on simplicity. When everyone on your team can understand what your goals are you have the maximum chance of success. Clarity rules. It makes evaluation more accurate, and when people understand with clarity, they will give more effort and focus. When you write out your goals (you *are* writing them down and making them public, right?) they should be one sentence, less than twenty words.

Measurable. This may be one of the biggest mistakes people make when setting goals. When? Where? How many? How soon? Compared to what? We will increase product X production by 10K units by June 30. On July 1 I can ask did production of product X increase by 10K? Most people hate this because now we have to be accountable for our performance. Here is the thing: goals are useless if we can't measure them and people aren't accountable. It's not fun calling out a team member in front of the whole team, but it has to be done if we are going to achieve our goals, and ultimately our vision. Now, you have to be clear to everyone that the goals are going to be measured and the team members will be responsible for their part ahead of time, not after the fact.

Attainable. This is tricky. What may seem to be attainable to me might not be to you. The challenge with whether something is attainable boils down to your willingness to make necessary changes to achieve something. For example, if a goal requires you to hire five more people and you are unwilling to do that, the goal is not attainable. My question would be whether attainability is based on a poorly written or conceived goal or your reluctance to do what is needed to achieve the goal. In most cases, speaking from personal experience, it is the latter. I will tell you that most times fear has been my worst enemy. Here is what I have discovered. Most concerns in this area are logistical in nature and can be dealt with. If all of the other criteria are positive, it's usually attainable if you are willing.

Relevant. Are your goals relevant? By this I mean, are they related to the success of your business? Of course your immediate answer is yes, absolutely. But, remember your dream, your vision? Do these goals serve that dream or have they been hijacked by something else? The end result, your vision, needs to dictate the incremental goals along the way. This is why it is so critical to review your vision, your purpose, and your core values regularly. Your goals are the servants of your *purpose* and *vision*, not the other way around.

Time Bound. I used to set goals at five year, or even longer, increments. What I discovered was I didn't have the stamina to keep the energy up for that long of a period. By year four or five things would start to fade and my energy started to wane. I decided to shorten my time frames to three years, then to one year. What I discovered was by doing this, the wins came sooner and I didn't have to artificially pump up our team. Over the last few years I have discovered an addendum to this idea. By creating quarterly goals, and even monthly ones, the sense of urgency is heightened and our focus is much narrower. We are giving more concerted effort and energy to fewer things at once, which is multiplying our efforts. There is, however, one small secret to compressing your time. When others are counting on us to complete our part we pay more attention and do whatever is necessary to complete it on time.

Goals are the markers that tell us whether we are on course or not. Goals give us a benchmark to know if our activities are helping or hurting us, but by themselves they are pretty much useless. Don't believe me? Have you ever set a personal or business goal and forgot about it? Yeah, me to. Why? Because there was no plan to implement activities and behaviors that would actually help achieve the goal. This is where systems and processes (my favorite subject) come into play. What are the leading indicators (activities) you will systematically implement in order to move toward the goal?

So how do we make goals effective? I love what Darren Hardy says here: "Forget about them." What? He's right. Yes, you need to have an awareness of your goals and what they are, but don't fixate on them. I have noticed that large, really big goals cause me to sort of freeze up. How about you? I become fixated to the point I start asking, "How am I going to do that? I don't think I can do that. Why did I set the goal so big?" What happens is the sheer size of the goal overwhelms my thinking. But, if I start building processes and systems and taking actions that will help me move toward the goal and keep my focus on them, I am not intimidated by the big goal. When I focus on the process and measure the incremental progress we seem to stay on track much better.

Let me illustrate this from my own personal life. In my early adulthood I worked in pretty physical situations and had little trouble keeping the weight off. As I got older my career choices became less physical and more mental. However, my eating habits didn't change and I didn't maintain the same level of activity, so you can probably guess what happened. Well, for several years I set goals to lose weight, and nothing changed. My goals were SMART and very on target. However, it wasn't until I changed my behavior and routine that things changed. Get up early, go to the gym, hire a trainer, find accountability partners, and most importantly, plan for better eating habits. All of these activities were part of a system and a process designed to reach my goal. I am happy to say I am now in

Hard Knocks

better health than I was twenty years ago. The goals were my benchmarks, but the system and process, and most importantly, the actions taken, made it happen.

Let me summarize the last few paragraphs like this: Dreams require goals to keep your course true and on target. Goals require processes, systems, and actions in order to be achieved. Your team needs to know they are improving, going in the right direction and having success in order for them to keep doing the behaviors and activities necessary to achieve the goals.

A side note here. Focus on the small wins along the way. It will keep your team engaged and it will take the stress off of you to keep the positive excitement going 24/7. When you see improvement, take note of it. When your team is working to achieve a goal and they make improvements but you seemingly ignore them, you demoralize your team. Regular success and the recognition of others on the team become contagious and a little addictive. Small successes breed bigger successes.

Conclusion

As you conclude this short journey I have several hopes for you.

First, I hope you will spend some time being honest with yourself and really discover not only who you are and what you believe, but really how much you know and how capable you are as a leader. Discover your most exceptional strengths and double down.

Second, I hope you will demonstrate real courage and start taking some calculated risks that you will push the edges of what is comfortable. You have some great ideas, courageously act on them and stop worrying about failure, because it isn't.

Third, I hope you will get out of your own way and let others participate in your entrepreneurial adventure. Become a leader who is clear about why you do what you do and how that will play out. Inspire others to join the "cause." Seek out the patriots who agree with your vision.

Finally, I hope when it gets hard you won't quit, because hard is part of the process. Make every choice count, especially the small ones, because they are the ones that will sneak up on you and undercut all the work you have done, or the ones that will suddenly, one day, surprise you. The consistent effort is worth it.

Don't be discouraged when people are messy. So are you. Guide and coach people toward their best self. Create systems and processes that provide the fence lines and then let people work within the boundaries to achieve more than you could have alone.

I honestly think each one of us has a story like this in us. We have lessons learned, mistakes made, successes achieved. What we do with those events depends on our mindset and willingness to be better, to improve and to lead more effectively. We can choose to let difficulties and successes slide into oblivion without a thought, or we can choose to capture each one and extract a lesson learned, apply it, and incrementally improve. I have chosen to capture as many lessons as possible from my mistakes and my successes. I choose to apply everything I can toward the goal of improving each day.

How about you? What lessons have you learned? What actions are you going to take to improve your business and your role as a leader? Do you have a group of business people who will challenge you to be a better leader? Do you have a plan, or will you make one now to restructure and delegate those things you are not exceptional in? Who do you need to recruit to your "cause," right now? There is no time like the present to start.

Have you begun to write down your values, those things that determine your decisions? Have you at least made some effort toward defining your purpose in this world? I have listed mine below as a sample to get you started. I challenge you to do this soon because it is the foundation of everything else you do. Get clear about this one thing and all else will be much easier and much more clear.

<u>What is my personal purpose?</u>

I inspire and influence positive change.

<u>What are my personal values?</u> (some of these may not make sense so I will editorialize in some cases.)

Love God, serve people.

Lean into the wind and keep moving.

> (Life is full of resistance, we can choose to push forward regardless, or we can allow the resistance to stall our progress.)

Burn the ships.

> (In 1519, Hernan Cortes ordered the burning of all ships, giving his men the only option, to conquer or die. Essentially, the idea is you are all-in as if your life depends on it.)

Never settle for average.

Be the exception.

Always be Learning (ABL)

Reject assessments, accept assertions.

> (Assessments are based in personal judgment and opinion; assertions are statements based in fact.)

Step into another person's shoes.

> (We are too quick to dismiss others. We need to stop and view the situation from their perspective.)

My hope is that in some way I have inspired and possibly influenced you to keep going or to take a new look at your circumstances and make some positive changes in your business, in your life.

About R Mike Derryberry

Mike Derryberry is the chief development officer and co-owner of Compass Cleaning Solutions, based in Phoenix, Arizona. Mike's previous businesses include a casework manufacturing company and a software consulting and training firm. He has a passion for small business owners and developing leaders who care about people as much as profits. His message is a practical "boots on the ground" call to all small business owners looking for a voice from one of their own.

www.ingramcontent.com/pod-product-compliance
Lightning Source LLC
LaVergne TN
LVHW041341080426
835512LV00006B/559